May your Life *be filled*

with Love

Faith

Fun

In Poetry

Marion Adams
McClanahan

Life Love
Faith
Fun

In Poetry

Marian Adams

LIFE LOVE FAITH FUN In Poetry
Self-published with Amazon
Copyright © 2015 by Marian Adams

ISBN:
13:978-1500495039
10:1500495034

Contents

Acknowledgements

This book would not have been possible without assistance from my friend, Kit Arbuckle, who selflessly gave of his experience and knowledge in answering my many questions about computer functions, enabling me to create a printable version of the vision I had for self-publishing a book of my poems. Kit's wife, Sharron, and their son, Daniel, also gave of their technical expertise to help with special parts of the graphics.

Although I had used a computer for over 25 years, I had just indulged in a new laptop, changed to a different word processor and decided to self-publish a book, this book, with Amazon. Any one of those components would have presented a challenge; audaciously, I had taken on all three. I am thankful for all those who have encouraged me and given me thoughts to stimulate my writing in rhyme.

Norene Harvey, a former student, now a special friend, kindly and carefully proofread the manuscript.

My dear friend and good neighbor, Pamela Rowland, has been a tremendous inspiration. She also photographed the author portrait.

The Holy Spirit breathes life into my creative thinking just when I think the flame is about to go out. I am eternally grateful.

Foreword

Although you may, this book was not designed to be read from cover to cover. It is a collection of poems, each one complete in itself. The Table of Contents arranges the poems under the themes in the book title: Life, Love, Faith and Fun. If perchance you are struggling with a decision, turn to a verse which expresses Faith. If a small group is conversing in fun-loving ways, open the book to the Fun section and read aloud something light-hearted. Life is an all-encompassing term for a myriad of everyday happenings.

Love is a magical, mystical, emotional and spiritual feeling which defies description. Composers of music and authors of poetry and prose have all tried to express the depth of this ethereal experience.

Life, Love, Faith and Fun are so intermingled that it is difficult to place in categories the verses describing them; thus, the cover, featuring a precious Chain of Love holding them loosely together.

Poetry is especially effective when read aloud, although doing so may require a little practice. Even very young children will usually respond joyfully to the meter and rhyme. It is hoped that as you pick up this book and read for a moment, you will find solace, peace, or a laugh, at just the right time in your busy life. And who knows? You may wish to try your hand at writing in verse.

Included is a section of verses in Japanese forms. The strict number of syllables and lines required, provides the challenge of presenting an idea using very few words.

If *"music soothes the savage breast"*, [1]
Surely, poetry feeds the hungry soul.

[1] William Congreve, playwright, from *The Mourning Bride, 1697*

Life

Life is a gift from our God and Creator.

Use it for evil and reap distress;
Use it for good and build success.

Marian Adams

Clouds

Clouds go floating,
Just like boating
On a beautiful blue velvet sea.
Some are wispy,
Some are crispy
As sand, when tide leaves the shore.
They may be fluffy,
Or at the very least, puffy,
Growing and changing in wind or lee.
Cirrus and stratus,
Cumulus and more,
Close your eyes and let dreams soar!

Around the Year [1]

January bleak;
Diversion from blandness seek.

February chills.
Frost and snow paint all the hills.

March lion roars rage,
Slinks when no longer on stage.

April opens earth.
Bulbs burst forth in timed rebirth.

May ushers color.
Blossoms adorn in splendor.

June is queen of all:
Love, romance, weddings on call.

July follows fast;
Activities too soon past.

1 "Around the Year" could have been placed in the section of Japanese Forms. It is written in the pattern of a Choka. Because of its length and subject matter, it seemed more appropriate to place it near the beginning of the book.

Marian Adams

August is hazy
With a pace that is lazy.

September brings change:
Weather, work, home from the range.

October is bright,
Most days sunny, one of fright.

November shows grace
For goodness in its embrace.

December shows love.
God came to earth from above.

Although chosen words are few,
Each month has been in review.

Seasons Come and Seasons Go

Seasons come and seasons go
Each with its moments of splendor.
Beginnings and endings are hard to know
So open your senses; enjoy all four.

Summer is for going and doing and growing.
Blossoms abound in every hue.
Tints and shades create a tapestry glowing
As each plant and flower takes a bow or a cue.

Autumn moves gradually in on the scene
With its dominant yellow, orange and red.
Leaves splashed with color, less of the green;
The earth gave its harvest and now goes to bed.

Marian Adams

Because winter is next with chills and thrills,
Wind, frost and raindrops here to predict
A landscape white and a box full of bills.
Celebrations are worth it, the people's verdict.

For some, the winter may seem very bleak,
For the young and athletic, pure pleasure.
There is skiing, snowboarding, not for the weak,
But majestic beauty abounds without measure.

As the last snows melt, a snowdrop peeps out.
The earth is alive as spring bulbs feel the sun
And all living things seem to stand up and shout,
"Life is eternal; the victory is won!"

Color by Season

Spring's color palette
Brings pretty light brights,
Alive and refreshing
After winter's long nights.

Summer's colors are faded,
Serene and calm.
Pastels and neutrals
Are a soothing balm.

Autumn's raging colors
Burst on the scene,
The brightest and deepest
Hues that have ever been.

Winter's striking contrasts
Are stunning to behold –
Black and white or gray,
Bright red and gold.

The Master Designer
Chose colors for us, too.
Hair, skin and eyes
Tell what season are you.

Marian Adams

Most amazing of all is this little tip:
Remember it well on your next shopping trip,
The colors you like are usually the colors that fit
Your personal color by season palette.

Are you a Spring? Summer? Autumn? Winter?

A Walk in the Park

I went for a walk in the park one day,
And what did I see along the way?
I saw a bumblebee buzzing, flying to pay
A visit to a rose; his work looked like play.

I heard a frog with a very, very loud croak
Near the pond, so often he could soak.
Step lightly; so this frog you do not provoke,
Or awaken the elves and the fairies, the wee folk.

Oh, yes, they very well could dwell
'Mid the wild flowers now blooming down in the dell.
Shush, and please don't go running pell-mell,
Listen, you just might hear the sweet sound of a bell.

I'm sure when all is quiet, with no one around,
The coral bells ring, lily of the valley, too, sound,
Snapdragons snap and tulips may kiss, I've found.
With all of these happenings, enough to astound,
A walk in the park can be exceedingly profound.

The frog stopped his croaking, but look at the pond!
The ducks now are swimming, they have a strong bond;
They all swim together, directed by an invisible wand,
Soundlessly moving, of watching them I'm truly fond.

Marian Adams

Next time I go I'll take mother and brother;
Lift up a rock and see what we discover.
All kinds of creepy, crawly things, oh, what a wonder.
Look under logs; see what you uncover.

Look up at the sky, see birds on the wing,
Beautiful butterflies out for a fling,
Squirrels flying and seeming to swing,
And remember,
Our God in heaven made you, me and everything!

Queen of the Flowers

Tea Roses are not difficult to grow.
Words to the contrary are simply not so.
Choose a sunny space for a bed or a row.
Thirty- to thirty-six-inch spacing will be apropos.

Perennial they are, but please remember this:
In northern climes, don't be remiss,
Plant deep, and cover with redwood mulch
Or leaves from your raking or from the gulch.

Cut bushes low
Before cold winds do blow.
In the spring prune hard,
This is no canard.

Remove all old canes, leave greenest three, five, or seven.
They will grow fast; you'll think they're growing to heaven.
Fertilize and water, not often, but deep,
Once a month do routine care. They grow while you're
asleep.

Marian Adams

In June when they bloom, roses will grace your estate.
Invite some of your friends, perhaps six or eight
To High Tea at Three held in honor of the Queen.
"Queen of what? Queen who?" your guests questions
pose.
"**Queen of the Flowers**, of course." The answer: **The Rose!**

Autumn Sunset

Like peach parfait
Tinted clouds seem to play,
Folding into lavender sugar on a tray.
      A sliver of moon is nearby.

Sunset is fading,
Dusk is invading
With tints and shades of blue braiding.
      The sliver of moon draws nigh.

The curtain falls
On nature's halls,
The skyline etched with stark silhouettes.
      The slender, silvery sliver of moon lights the sky.

Marian Adams

Seasonal Showtime

Summer fades;
Fall parades
Endless dark bright shades.

Blending to gray
Day by day,
Winter spreads a bright white way.

Spring emerges,
The whole world urges
A tapestry of hues in surges.

Summer blooms flair
Filling the air
With myriads of scents and shapes rare.

As Summer is fading
Fall begins its parading.
Showtime starts all over again.

Bonfire in the Fall

Big piles we'd been raking,
Houses and tunnels a-making.
Then jump and scramble;
But there was no mistaking
The fun of the frolic
Was well worth retaking.

The wind stirred the leaves
That fell to the ground
Or gathered in the eaves,
Some formed a mound.
The colors were stunning!
The big day was coming!

On Saturday next,
We knew the routine,
Rake one huge pile, (no need for a text),
Onto a specified green;
No more play as on a trampoline.
Just create the biggest pile anyone has ever seen.

Marian Adams

Savor the scent of leaves a-drying.
Well worth remembering, not for buying.
Chrysanthemums nearby add their spice;
Such an exotic brew worth twice the price.
'Twould make any witch quite an attraction
With stirring and costume, complete satisfaction.

The moment comes; Dad lights the fire.
Flames burst forth, going high and higher
Cutting the sky as they scare and dare.
The scent of burning is strong in the air.
Smoke curls in spirals; nothing can compare,
Of which I'm aware, to this day of flare.

As the pile burns down to a few lingering embers
Mom brings out the marshmallows, (she always
remembers),
To spear on the sticks Dad has been shaping.
Turn and watch them lest they burn in the baking,
A sweet reward with sights, scents, sounds – all
For this once-a-year ritual called "Bonfire in the Fall".

Grandma's Baking

Two cups of flour, the cracked teacup will enable.
Soda rounded just right using a teaspoon from the table.
A pinch of salt and a handful of love, would be just enough.
Dabs of lard and butter worked in with nimble fingers.
A bowlful of fluffy goodness, now crumbly and a bit rough.
Place another piece of wood, (grandma never lingers),
In the big old iron cook stove, which was keeping us warm
As we stood around watching, and listening to the storm.
Add buttermilk or sour milk to bring the dough together;
Knead it on the old breadboard 'til it's light as a feather.

Cut into rounds with an empty baking powder can.
Pop them in the oven. What's more tantalizing than
The aroma of baking biscuits, a sure to please plan?
"Are they done now, grandma?" the little voices yell
As grandma peeks in the oven, then opens it wide to see.
Golden mounds, popped on plates. Just follow the smell.
Slather with butter and jelly, both anticipated with glee.

Marian Adams

Breakfast next morning was always a treat!
Grandpa liked flapjacks, with sugar syrup sweet.
We children would wait until he had his fill,
Then grandma would add sugar to the tasty batter.
"May make you fatter, when young, what does it matter?"
She must have made extra, there was plenty to grill
Into fried cakes in small sizes, we knew the drill.
We thought we could eat dozens, dozens and dozens.
At least that was the aim of the visiting cousins
                 At grandma's house.

Recipe Drawer

See an inviting recipe;
Tuck it in a drawer.
Need an inspiration?
To the drawer explore.

This one may be a keeper,
That one just so – so.
Another may be a sleeper;
Try it, then you'll know.

At least it's a change,
Something new to taste.
Just so it's not really strange
Most families will not waste.

When hungry, we're not so discerning,
But slow down and truly enjoy.
It's all part of learning;
Taste buds and brain waves together employ.

And the next time the chef hears the call,
"What's for dinner?"
The answer is at the ready,
"I think I may have a winner."

Marian Adams

First Snowfall

Tiny snowflakes filled the sky surreptitiously,
A few at the beginning, gradually increasing.
Their production expanded expeditiously
And did not show signs of decreasing or ceasing.

The multitude created a veil of gray outside,
Tightly spaced and very highly synchronized
Else there would be danger that they would collide
And spoil the ballet, choreographed or improvised.

Hours passed; the flakes gradually grew in size,
Merging into intricate patterns, doilies in crochet,
Taking form right there in the darkening skies,
Falling faster with weight like a well-loaded sleigh,
Covering sleeping shrubs and trees with a blanket of white.
Midst contrasts stark, the snow softly tip-toed into the
night.

Figure Skating

I find myself completely mesmerized
Thinking of all each skater has memorized.
Each movement has to be actualized
And placed in the program carefully organized.
At the same time the music must be characterized;
All the sequences have to be conceptualized.
Each rehearsal and performance must be analyzed,
Even the slightest flaw thoughtfully agonized,
So that the whole can be timed and capsulized,
Ready for presentation, as in music, concertized.
All the while making it seem as if improvised
Or the program, possibly, totally extemporized.

Phew!

Marian Adams

Ice Dancing and Pairs

Ice Dancing and Pairs, in figure skating parlance
Are performed in defiance of gravity.

The entrants have an abundance of audacity
Backed up by ballet training in agility,
Else how could they ever avoid calamity?
They exhibit tremendous tenacity,
A pleasing display of vanity and humility,
Acting ability in projecting personality,
As the finished program exudes originality.

In reality all of this bridges on insanity,
Costumed beautifully with all movements in balance.

Rocks

Rocks make up a part of every terrain,
Some are gigantic, some are very small,
Some glisten in the sun, differently in the rain,
They may be in sheets or stand very tall.

Since the beginning of time man used rocks in construction
To make huge cathedrals and castles and bridges.
Many edifices have stood the test, avoiding destruction,
Marvelous to see standing high on scenic ridges.

Walls and floors can be beautifully defined
Without cutting or chipping, just natural stone,
Giant jig-saw puzzles using what nature designed,
Searching the stack to find the one unbeknown.

That certain one was the key, the work goes faster
As the eye sees the shape for which the next rock was cast.
The finished part looks like the work of a master.
The product will the creator outlast.
And knowing there never can be an exact copy,
The artistry will forever remain unsurpassed.

Marian Adams

Look to the Beech Tree

Do you ever feel as though you're standing alone,
Even though there are many people involved?
In the midst of discussing an issue the tone
Suddenly changed and a deafening silence evolved.

Think of the beech tree stretching to the sky.
Trees all around are growing branches that push.
The beech holds its ground, though weeping, no cry;
It would rather be a tree any day than a bush.

The beech tree is different in color and character,
In beautiful bronze, with stately demeanor.
So look to the beech tree, be yourself, your own way.
Say what you mean and mean what you say.

Seeing your valor your ideas may sway
Others to think deeply, their own thoughts to convey.
Contentment you'll find, alone or in a crowd;
Hold your head high and be justly proud.

Daily Life

When I was young,
       I could sing, I could dance,
Making it all up as if in a trance;
But as I grew older
       and took learning in stride
The me inside me just got pushed aside.
There were more and more "have tos"
And fewer dreamy "to dos", because
       Life is so daily.

Then came the goal of making a living,
And doing things for others
       is all about giving.
Marriage and a daughter
       require creative skill:
Cookery, sewing, God's love to instill,
With humility and diligence all every day.
But where was the me inside me tucked away, because
       Life is so daily?

Marian Adams

My dear friend and good neighbor,
    without saying a word
Caused me to think . . . . . now,
    I'm free as a bird!
Is the me inside me still tucked away
    in some very dark corner
    and can't come and play?
Or would it, like a chrysalis,
    burst open and reveal
A beautiful butterfly –
    words and tones with appeal?

Life is still daily;
    there's a yard and housekeeping
And I find that my body
    needs a little more sleeping.
My days will be fewer than
    I thought long ago
But I feel that the me within me
    is not faux.
I'll take it out gently, expose it to light
And see if the butterfly
    will delight to take flight . . . . .
        Daily?

Moon Dance

The cold winter moon
Cast its silvery light
And eerily lit up the room.
A scared little whimper
From a helpless babe
Brought mom quickly down the hall.
She cuddled her wee one
And walked through the house
To show her the source of the light.
What caught baby's gaze
Was a bright silver shape,
A reflection created by moonlight.

My little one squirmed to get down on the floor
And play with this newfound creature.
She traced it with her tiny fingers, tried to pick it up, too.
What a magnificent adventure!
She would stand and look at the sky,
Then plop – sit back on the floor.
Stand again; plop again.

Tiring of this game in the sweet by and by
With a bottle and cuddling
She soon went to dreamland.

Marian Adams

For mommy 'twas pure joy
To watch her toddler's fascination
With her enchanting newfound toy.

When she was a six-year-old child
We watched TV together
As Neil Armstrong and two astronauts
Landed on the moon and walked (with a tether).
They called it a walk
Though it looked like a weird dance
As weightless bodies tried to advance.
That great accomplishment was well earned;
And the happy celebration well deserved.

There have been many more moonlit nights,
Many other bright lights
That rose to great heights
Since that very first landing on the moon.
But nothing can ever compare
With the night, oh, so rare,
When my 15-month-old danced with the moon.

I Could, I Would, I Can

'T would be such a lark
    to run in the park
        were it not for my a-fibbing heart.

I would like to swing
    like a bird on the wing
        were it not for my a-fibbing heart.

I could go dancing
    with steps so enhancing
        were it not for my a-fibbing heart.

Leaves I could rake
    without even a break
        were it not for my a-fibbing heart.

I could cross-country ski,
    winter wonderland and me,
        were it not for my a-fibbing heart.

On the ice I would glide
    and gracefully slide
        were it not for my a-fibbing heart.

Marian Adams

I CAN walk every day
    see beauty along the way,
        just me and my a-fibbing heart.

Wish it would stop fibbing
    with all of it's a-fibbing
        and be a good little heart.

Blank Paper

I have before me a page of blank paper;
Whatever shall I write?
Perhaps writing should wait until later,
Then, I may think of something bright.

Ideas are often so fleeting,
Coming sometimes while I'm sleeping.
By morning the inspiration has vanished,
The idea and my Muse have been banished.

Blank paper is somehow intimidating;
It challenges me, actually, like a dare.
A dare is as traumatizing as a scare.
I find it frustrating, and as well, humiliating.

When truly inspired I'll find a scrap
Of paper with even a tiny space blank
And scribble illegibly in order to trap
The ideas flowing from my think tank.

I soon have the scrap filled and hunting for more.
I turn on the computer in order to store
And organize this sketchy mass of letters unlined,
And see signs they can be combined, aligned and refined.

Marian Adams

Perhaps I will learn someday to just start.
Choose a subject, an idea, a feeling from inside.
Something deeply buried within my own heart,
Something I am willing to confide, not hide.

I'll try that someday and perhaps feel the pride,
Enjoy the ride and the swell of the tide
Of words that spill out of my heart and my mind.
Someday I'll try that, when I feel so inclined.

Free-thinking People

Free-thinking people came to this shore
Risking their lives and possessions,
Taming the wilds, going to war,
New life and liberty became their obsessions.

It soon became clear
That to keep God-given liberty
And protect the people from fear
Needed was personal responsibility.

But if that was not enough
To keep human nature in line,
Limited government would surely rebuff
And peace and happiness allowed to shine.

To set up some order many groups wrote
Contracts, compacts or constitutions.
They elected administrators, people of note,
Directed by the people to enact solutions.

These small groups became the 13 sovereign states
Governed by the Articles of Confederation.
The weak central government focused the debates
On a strong U.S. Constitution, not more accommodation.

Marian Adams

This excellent document, now besmirched and ignored,
Largely not taught nor understood by "now" generations.
Say some, only fit to be archived and stored;
Others, original intent deserves applications.

The administration is tyrannical; the Congress is weak;
Election and the ballot box hold the strength that we seek.
It is up to all citizens to shout from the steeple,
"The strength of the nation is in its people."

Between Sunrise and Sunset

In the moments just before sunrise
When all life seems to stand still
Awaiting dawn and daytime guise,
Lifting darkness as sun ascends the hill,
'Tis then God's creation is in clear view
And mankind's activities begin to ensue.

The doves begin their mournful sound.
Aromas of coffee and bacon fill the air.
Cars are revving, to work they are bound;
A small stream of walkers gather here and there.
Life is busy and always on the move,
But not to be forgotten is God's great love.

The description above is more aptly applied
To small towns and cities across this our nation.
But what about the people who live side by side
In large cities, tall buildings, except for work or vacation.
Then, they may just fly over the beautiful expanses
Giving the wondrous resources below fleeting glances.

Perhaps all they see through a heavy sea of clouds
Is the paperback or ebook right in front of them.
If they could look through a magic lens, see the crowds,
Not of people, but of cattle, now there's a gem,
The source of hamburgers most like so well.
The thought sends the smell and hunger hard to quell.

Marian Adams

This flyover country holds most of the materials.
The people who live there know firsthand that reality.
An on-the-ground visit to these interesting locales
Would focus the realization of all people's commonality.
A visit to the big cities can be nothing short of surreal;
A visit to the heartland should have widespread appeal.

In large cities are seen not streams, but rivers of people;
Traffic jams are commonplace, accidents, too.
The smells are an odd mixture of foods and of diesel.
Sounds of this busyness are difficult to get through.

Understanding the necessity of these two ways of life,
One focused on humanity, the other on gifts of nature
Should help to keep the nation united without strife
And focused on the Creator instead of the creature.

No need for daylight savings time;
That is mankind's invent. Don't fret,
Day still awakens at sunrise prime
And ends with a glorious sunset.

Take Pride in America

Take Pride in America!
Land of the free.
America is the beacon
The whole world wants to see.
Take Pride in America!
Although that's just a start.
Take Pride in America!
Learn to do your part.

Learn the hist'ry of this great land,
Self-governance is the measure.
Vigilance will set it straight,
This nation is a treasure.

Perchance a tyrant wins the lead,
We must all be strong.
Stand for right and the "rule of law"
And fight to right the wrong.

Marian Adams

This nation's form is a Republic,
Representative and fair.
If every eligible citizen
Will study candidates with care.

Thank God for America!
The source of all creation.
The best of all He saved for us,
The heart of the land, our nation.
Thank God for the USA!
Now it's up to you and me
To fight for right
With all our might,
Right the wrong
To keep us strong,
And cherish **Liberty!**

The Changing of the Guard

Have you witnessed in awe the brief moments
When yesterday and today are both on display?
The moon is setting; the new day is dawning,
Each in its splendor, then continue on their way.
The moon seems so close when near the horizon;
The sun with its energy and color opens the day.
These are not opponents, but respected components
Of a masterfully designed universe set to convey
The Changing of the Guard – make way!
Hardly noticed by most, given little or no regard,
Except by a wandering minstrel, a romantic, or a bard.

Marian Adams

Music and Poetry

Music is composed of myriads of sounds
Intricately woven to convey emotions and presage.
Poetry is written using carefully chosen words
In rhythm and rhyme to tell the author's message.

Listen to music and how it seems to soar,
Reaching new heights, never experienced before.
The poet's lyrics touch the very depths of the soul,
Together with memories they create a new scroll.

There are songs without words and words without a song;
Each elicits moods, memories, and feelings lifelong.
Slow down the pace; keep these arts in embrace;
Make the world a more livable, loveable place.

If *"music soothes the savage breast"*, [1]
Surely, poetry feeds the hungry soul.

[1] William Congreve, playwright, from *The Mourning Bride, 1697*

Marian Adams

Love

Love dwells in the heart.

There are so many kinds;
Let's sort them out at the start.
Romantic love, true love finds.
Friendship is love.
Love for God, the Divine.
Family love holds us together.
Brotherly love binds kindred souls
in a common endeavor.

Marian Adams

Friendship

Friendship is sharing
Deep thoughts of caring,
Never competing,
Ever completing
The circle of loved ones
Kept close to the heart.

Candlelight

In the bygone days of long ago
When setting sun gave way to night,
Firelight and candle glow
Were necessary forms of light.

Firelight for reading,
Snug as a bug in a rug;
Candlelight for leading
Upstairs to bed with a hug.

Now we think of candle glow
As adding a special flair –
On a package, a ribbon and a bow,
Or a flower for your hair.

Saved for very special days,
Not an everyday household chore,
Candlelight speaks of romantic ways
And stories of love and lore.

Once hand-dipped with loving care,
Tapers short and tapers tall,
Now mass-produced for all to share
In shapes and colors to please one and all.

The dim light of candlelight speaks of romancing,
No matter the wind and the blustery weather,
Lovers whisper sweet things, step lightly, slow dancing;
In such ambience know only together, forever.

A Special Couple

I know a special couple
Who for all the world could be
A real live, living, breathing
Ken and Barbie.

They are tall and slender –
A perfect match.
She has long golden tresses;
He is dark, and handsome, too.
At that remark my grandma would say:
"Handsome is as handsome does."
No problem, Gram, he's a real fixit man.
They are both thoughtful and helpful besides.

The most remarkable part
About this admirable pair
Is that they are young at heart.
(I hope they won't care.)
They are probably of middle age,
If my experience is any gauge.
Their children are grown
And off on their own.

Marian Adams

So my Barbie and Ken
Get out of their den
And off on their Harley they go.
Perhaps just for a ride
Or west to the tide
In wind or rain they're together.
As long as that's true
And they are true blue
What could it matter – the weather.

This beautiful couple
I watch day by day,
What a model of love they portray.
I know that they pray,
I see them at play,
I know that for aye
They're together.

A Rose Jar

Memories tucked in your heart
Are like rose petals placed in a jar,
Always there when you need them,
Perhaps sweeter when remembered afar.

Gently, so gently shake them;
The scent will reward you well.
Fill the jar to the brim;
Memories will also swell.

The petals will dry and slowly fade;
Memories, too, lose their ardor.
Pleasure you'll find as you rouse and invade
The nooks and crannies where they harbor.

After many years of living and you are all alone
The petals in the rose jar cause you to reminisce:
The carefree times of youth, the stressful years of decision,
About romantic times, perhaps a kiss, moments of bliss.

Nostalgia is not always pleasant,
There are tearful times as well:
A sad goodbye, a loved one's death,
As memories cast their spell.

Marian Adams

All are intertwined in your heart of hearts,
All have given you strength to endure
And follow the plan God made just for you,
Though sometimes obscure, it is secure.

Keep the rose jar and your memories
So that they are just a thought away;
But close them away from prying eyes
Until a sight or a scent revives the ballet.

The Moon

Tonight the moon looked so wistful.
Are there no romantic lovers?
No one to break the mood tristful,
Finding a lost love which still hovers?

Look at the silvery shape, envision dreams,
Not of the past, but of a future which gleams
Of promise, new hope, all by the grace
Of the One who spoke the stars and planets in place.
And in that vision leave a space hidden from view
For that very special someone chosen just for you.

With two dreamy lovers, the moon, no longer wistful,
Beams its silvery glow on all who are blissful.

Marian Adams

A Sonnet

The maiden was enamored with her stalwart lover.
He could not hide his passion behind the furtive glance.
He whispered sweet nothings, though barely a murmur;
Her faint blush in answer, her eyes did enhance.
Meeting at parties and teas, though all right,
Did little to satisfy the longings they were feeling.
What could they do to remedy their plight
And still play the game, their true love concealing?
Perhaps he could come to her home to call;
He could thus meet her parents, and then –
He would ask for her presence at the very next ball.
They planned and they dreamed, but did not know when.
    They could slip away to the garden this very night,
      Just the two of them together in the moon's silvery light.

Roses, Roses, Roses

Roses are the lover's choice.
A stem or a bouquet needs no voice.
Red roses mean "I love you!"
Another color may be best if you're new.

So many varieties from which to choose,
Bi-colors and blends with which to confuse
The giver; but the recipient would surely enthuse
Over a stem of your choice and not refuse.

What could possibly be more elegant,
Though it might be taken as extravagant?
A bouquet of pink roses means sincerity,
With a bit of sophistication for clarity.

Yellow immediately spells happiness
Provoking a rollicking reception of gladness.
Take your pick of color, a gift of roses is sweet.
She's sure to remember you, next time you meet.

Marian Adams

When Lilacs Bloom

When lilacs bloom
There'll be no more gloom;
Gentle breezes waft their perfume.

Young men flirt by glancing,
Maidens by skipping and dancing.
'Tis the time of year for romancing.

Dresses of lilac are stunning,
Matching bonnets are cunning,
Leisurely walking down Main, no running.

Young birds faintly cheeping,
Trees in bloom gracefully weeping,
Wise old owl, his watch is keeping.

May welcomes the wren;
Wild flowers paint the glen,
When lilacs bloom in the spring, again.

Unforgettable

Lovers' first kiss,
First baby bliss,
First snowfall thrills
In spite of the chills.

Daffodils bring
Longing for spring.
Bowers of flowers
Follow the showers.

Summertime fades
Amid autumn shades.
Celebrations abound
As year's end comes around.

No need to lament,
Capture each moment,
Filling every nook
Of your Memory Book.

Marian Adams

The Language of the Heart

LOVE – young love, true love,
Comes but once in its most passionate form,
Before the challenges and many distractions
Which can easily stir up a stressful storm.

What if the loved one doesn't call?
Tears well up quickly, ready to fall.
When the call comes, the flips begin,
Sending the heart into a spin.

The sound of the beloved's voice
Sets the mood to rejoice –
"When may I see you again?
When? When? Oh, when?"

Love is a mystery!
Who holds the key
As to why the heart skips,
Even does some back flips?

In all the world's history
Answers long held in secrecy.
'Tis all just a magical, mystical part
Of the intimate Language of the Heart.

Marian Adams

Faith

"Now faith is being sure of what we hope for
and certain of what we do not see."[1]

"We live by faith, not by sight."[2]

1 Heb. 11:1 (NIV)

2 II Cor. 5:7 (NIV)

Marian Adams

Help

Love can be fickle;
Jealousy is cruel.
Warring thoughts within us fuel
The fire that starts a duel.

Relationships are fragile,
Friendship is frail;
But the grace of God is constant,
Never will it fail.

Keep your thoughts on heaven
Where evil cannot assail.
Seek Him whose help is certain;
His guidance will prevail.

A Rudderless Skiff

Life is like a rudderless skiff
Blown here and there by the winds on the sea
Without so much as a sail to guide
The way for the helpless onboard, you and me.

The waves rise high in a troubling pitch
Like the problems faced almost daily;
Then down they go to the depths it would seem,
Smooth sailing is something seen rarely.

Just at the thought, "I can stand no more."
A peace over all fills the air.
The great God above is the anchor in charge;
He knows every unspoken prayer.

The idea of a mast causes a look below deck;
A shirt shall be the sail!
With Christ's steady hand and urging "Press on",
No peril can cause one to fail.

Marian Adams

And suddenly, there on the horizon,
A fleet of ships short and tall.
Each could contribute in some special way;
They willingly heed the call.

So with the omnipotent God the anchor,
Christ the model and guide,
The Holy Spirit is the rudder,
Fellow believers will come alongside.

A Special Place

Sound is all

Around, and I have

Found that there is solace in the calming of the

Heart, to go

Apart, right from the

Start, into a place safe and tranquil in His

Arms where no

Alarms or worldly

Charms can take away this special time of no more

Care, just words to

Share and blissful

Prayer time with **God.**

Read His word and think what He said.
What does it mean for me?
"Go, precious one, and tell the world
What I have done for thee."

Marian Adams

Sing the story!

Ring the glory!

Wing it on its way throughout the world where people

Long to hear your

Song of love. Be

Strong to tell how Christ died to pay the price to

Lift man from sin's

Rift with God's great

Gift and all its pow'r to give eternal life and

Save the weak or

Brave when God for-

Gave. **Praise the Lord**!

Oh, to see His face,

Know His saving grace,

Amen.

What Is Time?   Ecclesiastes 3: 1-8

Like the wind,
Time cannot be seen.
An illusion of the mind?
Shown on a screen?

The 4th dimension it is —
(A good answer on a quiz).
An interval perceived;
In music the pulse received.

Mankind has been fascinated
Since the beginning of time,
One might say captivated,
Trying to measure its prime.

Sundials were the first
In many civilizations.
Variations everywhere quite unrehearsed,
All to tell time, the goal of these aspirations.

Clocks were designed in practically all nations;
Everyone could have one, tell time at home.
Makers eager to show their latest innovations,
Made clocks to order – no need to roam.

Marian Adams

Then came personal time, watches to wear:
Pocket watches, wristwatches, brooches and more.
Timepieces to have with you, tight schedules to bear,
Stylized and colorized to match what one wore.

Until the 1960s a dial was the norm,
With marks for the hours and sixty minutes.
Then, digital was introduced, a very new form
With date and day, really testing the limits.

And now it isn't hard to find among youth
One who cannot tell time with dial or clock.
Analog is old-fashioned and quite uncouth;
Digital is the latest to read and in talk.

So, we have time on our hands, wrists, if you will.
Time relates to intervals in space which elapse.
We speak of the past, present and future, and still,
There's no travelling back or to the future with maps.

We live in the present, a moment, held in time's thrall.
Our mind stores up memories which we can recall.
We can dream of the future but cannot it forestall;
Only God, time's Creator, knows the end of it all.

One Morning

One morning I awakened in time to see
Strata of clouds in vivid vermillion.
What if this magical sight had escaped me?
A morning among mornings – one in a million.

And what a wonder to know that all through the night
The master painter, creator, had been planning this sight
To remind all of His children that He never does sleep,
But keeps watch over all, our souls thus to keep.

Marian Adams

October Sunrise

After a week of rain and gray scale skies,
Fluffy pink clouds gave the world a new glow
On a background of blue, a majestic surprise,
Defying description, but reminiscent of van Gogh.

A thin, pale veil of ochre hangs like a reverie,
It's the fall burning of leaves time of year.
Colorful leaves, touched as if by a Valkyrie,
Gently swirl and glide within their special sphere.

How can this beauty be surprising to view,
When the God of the universe performs miracles each day?
Know solace in His faithfulness to me and to you,
His promise to be with us through trouble along life's way.

"And surely I am with you always, to the very end . . . . . "[1]
So says Christ Jesus, our Savior, Redeemer and Friend.

1 Matt. 28: 20b (NIV)

Do We?

Do we lighten the load others are bearing?

Do we heighten the expectation of sharing?

Do we frighten by being too daring?

Do we brighten the day with our caring?

Do we tighten the rein on tongues flaring?

Do we slighten the showing and wearing?

Do we righten the wrongs that are glaring?

Do we whiten with kindness unsparing?

Do we?   Do I?

Marian Adams

Turkey's in the oven, lightly browned.

Hugs of welcome given all around.

All loved ones here at this table;

No one needs a special label.

Knowledge and wisdom we all seek:

Sacrifice self, be always meek,

Giving your best every day,

Ideals of the highest to portray.

Victory through Jesus we proclaim!

Identify with Christ without shame.

Nor forget to God to pray

Gratitude in humility every day.

AMEN.

Thanksgiving Menu

Prayer

We thank Thee, O God,
For the bounty here spread.
To Thee we give honor, glory and laud,
Lest we forget, when we are well fed.

Salad

A cornucopia of fruits;
At the table no one refutes.

Turkey

The noble entrée
In grand array for display.

Cornbread Dressing

What a blessing!
The favored dish of some, I'm guessing.

Savory Gravy

Not lumpy, but tasty,
Perhaps wavy – maybe.

Sauce

It's the cranberries!
In regal red, the day carries.

Dessert

Apple, Mincemeat or pumpkin pie!
For your favorite, please say, "Aye".

Marian Adams

The Day After Thanksgiving

The day after Thanksgiving I looked all around
And saw stacks of dirty dishes, enough to confound!
But having family and friends was one of my wishes;
So, in gratitude I'll wash them and shine them so bright
They'll be ready and waiting for Holy Christmas night.
What's that I see on the floor?
Some bedraggled leaves walked right in the door.
The vacuum will gobble them now that they're dry;
The floor will shine in no time, no need to cry.
Look at the lawn! It is swept clean.
The children must have raked; the rain made it green.
The next time they come everything will be white,
Just snow to track in, I must get the rug
To soak up the water and keep everything snug.
I'm already looking forward to their arrival at night
Singing "Silent Night" and shouting MERRY CHRISTMAS
tonight!

A Hymn

Christ Jesus is our Lord and King,
No other name can save us.
God sent His Son, His chosen one,
His name, of course, is Jesus.

This Jesus lived with men on earth
To teach mankind God's message:
"Love one another as yourself",
And give believers courage.

Christ Jesus is our Lord and King,
No other name can save us.
God sent His Son, His chosen one,
His name, of course, is Jesus.

Born in a manger, soft in the hay,
A star did mark His coming.
The angels sang until break of day,
Shepherds bowed 'mid humming.

Christ Jesus is our Lord and King,
No other name can save us.
God sent His Son, His chosen one,
His name, of course, is Jesus.

Marian Adams

Three Wise Men came from far off lands,
His star had sent them searching.
Wise men still follow His commands
Find Love can heal all hurting.

Christ Jesus is our Lord and King,
No other name can save us.
God sent His Son, His chosen one,
His name, of course, is Jesus.

The powerful saw Him as a threat;
This Jesus would their world upset.
They nailed Him to that awful tree
Whereon He died for you and me.

Christ Jesus is our Lord and King,
No other name can save us.
God sent His Son, His chosen one,
His name, of course, is Jesus.

Christ died to save us from our sin,
Then sent the Holy Spirit
To guide believers throughout life,
Salvation to inherit.

Christ Jesus is our Lord and King,
No other name can save us.
God sent His Son, His chosen one,
His name, of course, is Jesus.

The Miraculous Birth

Celebrate the Holy miraculous birth
With joyous exaltation, extraordinary mirth.
God sent His Son to live with mankind on earth.

Born to be King,
Angels did sing,
Gifts some would bring.

Gifts are fondly given to those whom we love,
But the greatest gift of all is the one from God above.
Jesus, the Christ, taught how to live, love and all thereof.

Lord of lords,
Harps sound chords,
His majesty accords.

Wise men still seek Him and believe in His name.
Salvation, God's gift to men, not wealth nor fame,
All wait for His Kingdom to come with final acclaim.

Alleluia! Alleluia! Alleluia all exclaim!

Marian Adams

Bells, Bells, Bells

Bells in the steeple
Ring for all people.

Hand bells ring in a choir
Of them, nevermore tire.
Sleigh bells ring in the snow,
Celebrate joy, faces aglow.
Church bells call all to raise
Voices in adoration and praise.
Silver bells ring of Christmas joy.
Used in décor, their glitter employ.
Bells ring warning, a clear alarm.
People must move away from all harm.
Carillons send melodies, clear in the air,
Calling to classes or calling to prayer.
Bronze bells produce the best sound of all,
Proven in the historic bells on this terrestrial ball.

C Christ Child, born in a manger,
      No stranger, our Savior.

H Holy One,
      God's only Son!

R Ruler over all, King of kings,
      Lord of lords.

I Inexpressible Joy filled hearts.
      Love to all He imparts.

S Shepherds came for themselves to see
      And worshiped on bended knee.

T Traveling far, Wise Men came,
      Following the light of the star.

M Mary adored Baby Jesus
      And pondered and wondered.

A Angels sang "Alleluias"
      At His birth.

S Savior long-promised
      Has come to earth.

Marian Adams

Christmas Eve

By late afternoon the baking is done
And all of the do-a-heads safely stored.
Seems all day everyone has been on the run
Finishing decorations, wrappings, looking toward
The Christmas Eve service, we're thinking in accord.
Time to get ourselves ready in our brightest and best
To celebrate God's gift to mankind, heaven blest.
As we're driving to church the snowflakes start falling,
The church bells are ringing, chiming and calling:
"Come to the manger where the Baby Jesus is sleeping."
Shepherds and wise men, their watch are keeping.
The sweet smelling hay is the stable's greeting.
Hear the angels singing as the hours are fleeting.
Listen to the story told over and over again
As it penetrates hearts with "good will to men".
Time to light the candles as we sing "Silent Night",
Then into the darkness to find everything white.
Home is so beautiful, love fills it bountifully.
With hugs and kisses, voices proclaim delightfully,
MERRY CHRISTMAS!

God sent His Son to be our Savior, Redeemer and Friend!

Wishing for Love

Possibly that is the wrong action.
Be likeable, loveable, a calming attraction.
Love at first sight may not be wise.
Look all around you and open your eyes
To the friends you have and those you meet.
You may very suddenly realize
There is someone you really should reach out and greet.

Getting better acquainted is a good place to start
Before even considering letting go of your heart.
What do your do for outdoor exercise?
What do you like to collect and to keep?
What is your vision for future enterprise?
What are the values you hold fast and deep?

Love grows and develops as commonality aligns
Good friends become lovers along those designs.
What is your faith? Do you express it in prayer?
That is a special question; the answer you should share.
Romantic love alone can be very shallow.
True love, like God's love, is to trust and to hallow.

Marian Adams

Reflections

December 31st, New Year's Eve!
Ring out the old but do not grieve;
Ring in the new
With an optimistic view.
Some people save fireworks from the 4th of July.
Oh, how they light up the clear, cold winter sky.
Save gladsome memories
For those someday reveries.
Look to the New Year as a great adventure;
Give it your all, not just a gesture.
Know that God placed you where He wants you to be.
Seize opportunities, pray for His Will, there's the key
To a life well-lived, lived purposefully.

Marian Adams

Fun

That which incites exuberant joy,
jubilant, spontaneous merriment.

Marian Adams

Words

Words tease me,
Words please me,
Words can appease me,
But not for long.

I have to be working,
Never to be shirking,
To see what is lurking
Behind every thought.

And if it's insulting
Without even consulting
The decision resulting
Will not withstand.

Rhyming Nonsense

If you've ever been rejected,
You probably felt dejected,
Almost like being ejected
Right out of your seat.

If a plan has been projected,
And you've tried to stay connected,
Although you've been properly subjected,
That probably suggests retreat.

If I err, please see I'm corrected.
May you never feel neglected
Unless you've really disconnected
And it's all going down to defeat!

One Whale of a Cloud!

I saw a whale in the sky last eve,
A large threatening cloud of darkest gray,
Barely moving on the pale sky taking leave,
As it silently plied the bay.

The shape was so whale-like I could easily imagine
The whale diving and breaching and spouting away.
Perhaps there was a young whale slightly submerged,
Protected and nourished, asleep or at play.

The whale soon blended with other dark shapes –
Whales in the distance – and floated away.
"That was one whale of a cloud!"
Was all I could think of to say.

Wild Wind

A certain lady carefully showered, shampooed and
styled,
Then entered the car to go to the store.
Out at the mall, the wind was wild.
It whooped up a terrible roar
And messed up her beautiful hair,
No longer finished with care,
People began to stare.
The lady exclaimed, "It's not fair!"
And where is her glamorous hair?
"Gone with the Wind".

(It's an ill wind that blows no good.)

Marian Adams

Medical Forecast

Because of the explosion in the activity of text,
Here's a prediction of what could happen next.
Instead of carpal tunnel being a most common repair
It's more likely to be thumb surgery due to repetitive wear
and tear.
In former times, before common use of machines,
Many tasks were performed using nimble willing hands.
Now, although they do not have to, so many teens
Are endangering their thumbs, as this activity expands.

Adults, too, are addicted to this risky behavior.
Just wait, we'll soon hear of the pain caused by failure
To limit the time spent curled up in a corner.
Proper exercise and rest are heeded no longer.

Thumb surgery may be required to repair the damage;
Both thumbs may be bound up in a cast and a bandage.
So, abandon this excessive, obsessive fixation,
Enjoy other forms of more personal communication.

Modern Technology

A pet peeve to be sure,
Especially the sound.
Aesthetics are forgotten,
Just take a look around.

Piles of cords here,
Black boxes over there.
I think to myself, nothing to fear;
Sit back and watch, I might even stare.

Here comes a "techy" so small, so lithe.
He looks like a mosquito caught in mid-flight.
Confidence exuding, attitude blithe.
He changes this, connects that, just right?

Someone adds something; perhaps that will do.
No. Unwrap some packages, boxes galore.
Two laptops are needed and two speakers too.
Never enough tables, he works on the floor.

Marian Adams

Amid all the mess how to know when it's done?

Or like big boys with toys is it all just for fun.

Test it; turn power on, and out comes a blare.

Time's up. Presenter enters. BUYER BEWARE

Molly and the Holly

Molly went to the mall
To buy holly to decorate the hall.
Wouldn't it be jolly
To have some holly
And then have a wonderful ball?

The first shop had no holly;
The next had only a dolly.
So, thought Molly
"This is no folly."
And so she continued her volley.

At the flower shop Molly met Holly.
Holly said it was too early for holly.
But that didn't stop Molly
Who wanted real holly,
No matter the desperation of Holly.

Marian Adams

Along the way she met Polly.
Polly might know of some holly.
"I do", said dear Polly;
"Come with me", dear Molly,
"I'll cut some for you, it's getting squally".

Polly had been pruning her holly;
Cut branches lay strewn in her yard.
So Molly had her holly;
Polly had no need to discard.
Molly with the holly went home on the trolley.

I forgot -- please accept my apology.

Molly and Polly live in Nisqually, (WA),
With their husbands, Pauli and Wally.
Molly decorated the hall
And had a great ball
In spite of the weather which was squally.

Fun   93

Little Day Moon

The little day moon
Looks like a balloon
A child let go of its string.

While walking along
Singing a song,
Balloon took off on the wing.

Now it romps with the clouds,
Moving in crowds, creating shrouds,
Now visible again in the ring.

When night rolls around
It's nowhere to be found;
On the other side its visage will swing.

Marian Adams

Images in the Sky

I saw a salmon in the sky this eve;
The color and detail were amazing.
The little fish swimming just below
Mesmerized me; I could not stop gazing.

The salmon morphed into another form –
A shrimp with a fan-like tail of gold.
Streamers were whirling and swirling around,
A magically gorgeous sight to behold!

And then at the end, as the clouds disbursed,
I saw a fish skeleton; I could count the bones.
I looked and I looked but never did find
The culprit, a cat named Stones.

A Recipe

Alternate dollops of yogurt in a bowl of pale blue.
Blueberry and nectarine will make the right hue.
Continue to fill the bowl and what will you get?
A healthy, light dessert, mirroring a stunning sunset.
Serves six or eight guests, 'twill disappear in an instant,
Timed as the clouds become more and more distant.

Marian Adams

Euphonious Sound

A Rainy Day Choral Reading

Count in four. Add a new voice after four counts.

1   2   3   4

	1	2	3	4
Voice i	Drip		Drop	
Voice ii	Drip	Drop	Drip	Drop
Voice iii	Drip Drop Drip Drop Drip Drop Drip Drop			
Voice iv	Splish		Splash	

Continue together 4 times gradually speaking more loudly.
Continue together 4 times gradually speaking more softly.

All voices: Stop (softly)

Optional endings:

Each voice drops out one at a time i-iv
Each voice drops out one at a time iv-i.

Marian Adams

Japanese Forms

Haiku
Tanka
Choka

Marian Adams

Light

Light in the room changed
From dark and rain to sunshine.
A rainbow appeared!

Good Intentions

A salad garden!
Lettuce, carrots, beets and chard.
Alas, did not plant.

Halloween

Halloween is here!
The scarier the better.
Dressing up is fun!

H
a
i
k
u

Springtime Trilogy

I

Trees in grand array;
tulips present their ballet.
Was that a raindrop?

II

It's May Day, my dear,
enjoy bowers of flowers.
Quickly fly the hours.

III

New shoots are greeting –
tints and shades, green and auburn
gone – the deer ate them

Marian Adams

Fall Mall Ball

Fall colors call all –
red, orange, yellow, purple –
have ball at the mall.

Spring Light Brights

Spring sights are light brights –
hyacinths, tulips, jonquils.
Rain washes them clean.

Summer Pastels

Summer stars pastels,
faded by sun's heat and light.
Cool colors refresh.

Winter Contrasts

Winter's white contrasts
bare branches and evergreens.
Now everything's white.

Wind

Wind can be gentle;
Wind is sometimes very wild.
If harnessed, it works.

Evergreen

Named Weeping Thread leaf,
an eye-catching evergreen
has a bad hair day.

Fire

Fire can be helpful.
Wild fires cause great destruction.
Smoke paints the sunset.

Marian Adams

Almighty God

Almighty Creates;
Due praise, honor and glory
Forever. Amen.
Author, redeemer and friend
Bless the Lord, my soul. Amen.

Hummingbird

Early one morning
Wee bird looked in the window.
"Where is my nectar?"
"Cooling. It will appear soon."
Hummingbird soon flew away.

Sunset

God is a painter:
Clouds of nectarine color
On a pale blue sky,
Brushed into gray ascending,
Send us an ominous threat.

T
a
n
k
a

Wedding Flowers

Blooms of red and blue;
Yellow completes every hue.
God blends them just right;
Creates a glorious sight.
How to choose for a wedding?

Marian Adams

Summer Storm

Wind and thunder first
Building to torrents of rain.
Trees bend with the storm;
Fires are contained with water.
Air smells fresh and clean.
Grateful for blessings of rain
The earth is at peace again.

Choka

About the Author

Marian Adams has lived a life of variety. A native of Washington State, born and reared in Spokane, she graduated from the University of Washington with a B. A. in Music and minors in English Literature and Education. After teaching for several years in small communities in the state, she married a Texan with a degree in Agriculture. The next forty years were spent growing apples and hay on scenic property along the Okanogan River. A daughter was born during those years who still lives near the former home place. Marian continued to teach privately, piano, flute and voice, and more recently, direct a hand bell choir in a community church. Memories of the many experiences she has had and the people who have touched her life inspire her to write; thus, the potpourri of verses you hold in your hand: Life, Love, Faith, Fun In Poetry. Also included is a section of poems in Japanese forms.

Alphabetical Index

Who? Me?

You may be a poet
And do not yet know it.
So here are some pages;
Write your thoughts for the ages.

They may be like a seed
From a beauteous plant or a weed.
But who knows? They may grow
Into something the whole world wants to know.

40109615R00083

Made in the USA
Charleston, SC
26 March 2015